Geoff Petrie

THE STORY OF THE PORTLAND TRAIL BLAZERS

Jusuf Nurkić

A HISTORY OF HOOPS

THE STORY OF THE

PORTLAND
TRAIL BLAZERS

JIM WHITING

CREATIVE SPORTS

Damian Lillard

CREATIVE EDUCATION / CREATIVE PAPERBACKS

Published by Creative Education and Creative Paperbacks
P.O. Box 227, Mankato, Minnesota 56002
Creative Education and Creative Paperbacks are imprints of
The Creative Company
www.thecreativecompany.us

Design and production by Blue Design (www.bluedes.com)
Art direction by Rita Marshall

Photographs by AP Images (Associated Press, Gene Puskar), Corbis (Paul
Benoit, Steve Dipaola, Steve Lipofsky, Chris Szagola), Getty (Andrew D.
Bernstein, Steph Chambers, Steve Dykes, Focus On Sport, Sam Forencich,
John Gress, Thearon W. Henderson, John Iacono, Walter Iooss Jr., Alika Jenner,
Fernando Medina, Manny Millan, Katelyn Mulcahy, Layne Murdoch, Joe
Murphy, Thomas Oliver, Jayne Kamin-Oncea, Ezra Shaw), © Steve Lipofsky,
Newscom (Ting Shen/Xinhua/Photoshot), USPresswire (David Butler II)

Library of Congress Cataloging-in-Publication Data
Names: Whiting, Jim, 1943- author.
Title: The story of the Portland Trail Blazers / by Jim Whiting.
Description: Mankato, Minnesota : Creative Education and Creative
  Paperbacks, 2023. | Series: Creative Sports: A History of Hoops |
  Includes index. | Audience: Ages 8-12 |
  Audience: Grades 4-6 | Summary: "Middle grade basketball fans are
  introduced to the extraordinary history of NBA's Portland Trail Blazers
  with a photo-laden narrative of their greatest successes and losses"--
  Provided by publisher.
Identifiers: LCCN 2022016853 (print) | LCCN 2022016854 (ebook) | ISBN
  9781640266414 (library binding) | ISBN 9781682771976 (paperback) | ISBN
  9781640007826 (pdf)
Subjects: LCSH: Portland Trail Blazers (Basketball team)--History--Juvenile
  literature.
Classification: LCC GV885.52.P67 W453 2023 (print) | LCC GV885.52.P67
  (ebook) | DDC 796.323/640979549--dc23/eng/20220523
LC record available at https://lccn.loc.gov/2022016853
LC ebook record available at https://lccn.loc.gov/2022016854

C. J. McCollum

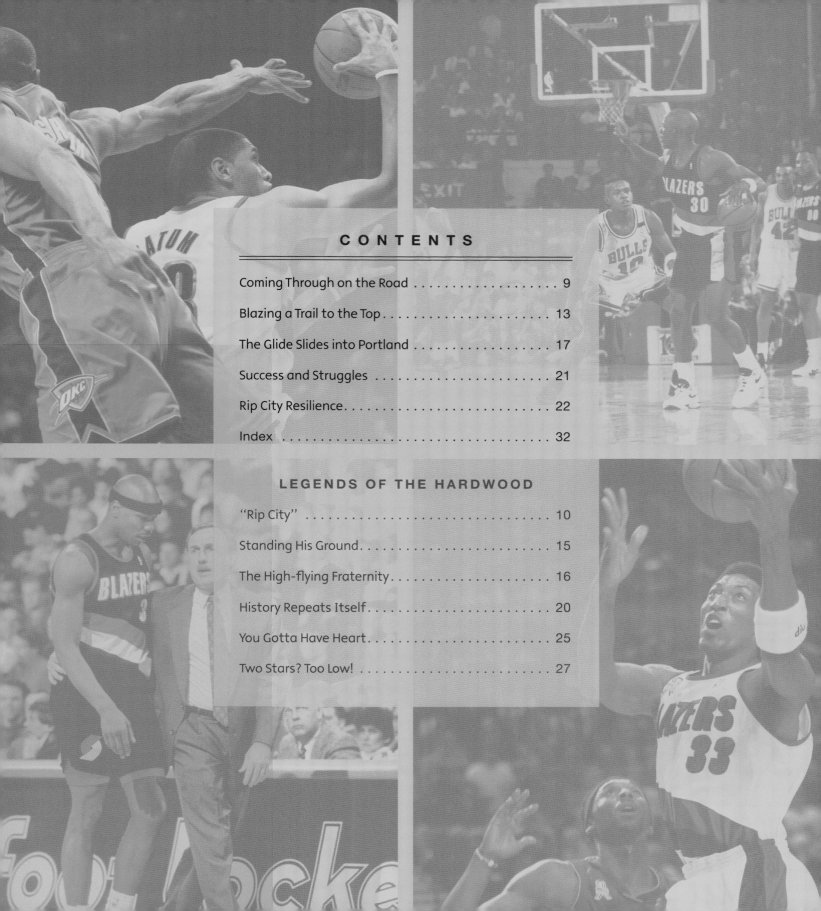

CONTENTS

LEGENDS OF THE HARDWOOD

C. J. McCollum

COMING THROUGH ON THE ROAD

The Portland Trail Blazers faced a difficult challenge in the 2019 Western Conference semifinals of the NBA (National Basketball Association) playoffs. The series was tied at three games apiece. Portland traveled to Denver to face the Nuggets in the decisive Game 7. Teams had won a Game 7 on the road only about 20 percent of the time. Portland had yet to accomplish that feat.

Midway through the second quarter, Portland trailed by 15 points. The Blazers reduced the margin to nine points at halftime. They completed their comeback with 12 seconds left in the third quarter. Guard C. J. McCollum drained a five-foot jump shot to give Portland a 72–71 lead.

The fourth quarter was tight. Guard Damian Lillard put Portland up by seven with a three-pointer with 3:20 left. Denver pulled to within 2 points with 11 seconds remaining. Portland guard Evan Turner drew a foul. He sank both shots. A desperation Denver three-point attempt didn't fall. Turner hauled in the rebound. Portland won 100–96. For the first time in 19 years, they would return to the conference finals! "This is arguably the biggest win we've had in the franchise in a long time, and to be a part of it, to do it the way we did, I'm thrilled," coach Terry Stotts said. "I'm really happy for our guys."

The city of Portland was happy for the huge win, just as they had been excited when the NBA granted it an expansion franchise in 1970. A name-the-team

Bill Walton

"RIP CITY"

During their first season, the
Blazers were playing the Los
Angeles Lakers. Blazers' guard Jim
Barnett drained a long jump shot. Radio
play-by-play announcer Bill Schonely shouted,
"Rip City—all right!" Scorekeeper Jeff Wohler asked
him where the phrase came from. Schonely replied,
"I don't know—it just came out." Wohler said, "Well,
leave it in." The phrase quickly became a symbol of
the franchise and the city of Portland. "Rip City"
T-shirts and other apparel are best sellers in the
official team store. Schonely retired in 1998. Yet
today he is still referred to as "the mayor of Rip City."

contest attracted more than 10,000 entries. Team officials went with Trail Blazers. The name referred to the Lewis and Clark expedition. It had passed through the region in 1805. "It really wasn't very popular when fans first heard it, but of course we all know that changed," said club executive Harry Glickman. Many people shortened it to Blazers. Terms such as "Go Blazers," "Blazermania," and "Rip City" quickly caught on.

The Blazers won just 29 games in 1970–71. The following season they slipped to 18 victories. They did have winners of the NBA Rookie of the Year in back-to-back seasons: sharpshooting guard Geoff Petrie in 1971, and versatile forward Sidney Wicks in 1972. But there wasn't enough talent surrounding them. The Blazers continued to finish at the bottom of the Western Conference. Many of their draft choices didn't work out as they had hoped.

BLAZING A TRAIL TO THE TOP

The 1974 NBA Draft was a different story. The Philadelphia 76ers finished last in the Eastern Conference. The Blazers sat at the bottom of the Western Conference. The teams flipped a coin to see who would choose first. The Blazers won. They took UCLA center Bill Walton. He was a three-time College Player of the Year. Portland fans expected immediate success. They didn't get it. Walton struggled with injuries. At various times he broke his nose, foot, and wrist. "For two years, I wasn't able to run up and down the court freely without … thinking about [my injuries]," Walton explained. He played just 35 games as a rookie and 51 the following season.

In 1976, Portland hired no-nonsense coach Jack Ramsay. He emphasized defense and a team-first attitude. He also benefited from the support of the "Blazermaniacs." They believed in the team, even though the Blazers still hadn't had a winning season. "The whole atmosphere in Portland was a huge psychological lift for me and the players," Ramsay said. Walton was finally healthy. Portland won 49 games in 1976–77. It was the team's first winning season. The Blazers cruised through the Western Conference playoffs. They defeated the Chicago Bulls and the Denver Nuggets in the first two rounds. Then they swept the Los Angeles Lakers in the conference finals.

The Philadelphia 76ers won the first two games of the NBA Finals. The Blazers crushed them in the next two. Portland opened up a 22-point lead early in the

Bill Walton

Maurice Lucas vs Darryl Dawkins, 1977 Finals

fourth quarter in Game 5. A furious Philadelphia rally fell just short. The Blazers won 110–104. More than 5,000 fans greeted the team at the Portland airport at 4:30 the following morning. "When we got off that plane and we saw the level of support and the level of commitment, there was no way we were ever going to give up," said Walton.

In Game 6, the Blazers jumped out to a 15-point halftime lead. Philadelphia closed to within two points with eight seconds left. A Philadelphia player fired up a potential game-tying shot. No good. Another shot. No good. A third shot. Still no good. Walton controlled the rebound as time ran out. The Blazers were NBA champs! Walton ripped off his jersey and hurled it into the stands at Portland's Memorial Coliseum. "If I had caught the shirt, I would have eaten it," said teammate power forward Maurice Lucas. "Bill's my hero."

MAURICE LUCAS
POWER FORWARD
HEIGHT: 6-FOOT-9
TRAIL BLAZERS SEASONS:
1976–80, 1987–88

STANDING HIS GROUND

Officially, Maurice Lucas was a rookie when he joined the Blazers. But he had already played two years in the American Basketball Association (ABA) before it folded. He gained a reputation as an enforcer. An enforcer is a player who physically supports his teammates. "There's nobody can contest him inside," said teammate Bill Cartwright. "Anybody tries, they're going to be in a lot of trouble." Lucas was a three-time All-Star. He teamed with Bill Walton to form one of the league's best frontcourt combinations. They led Portland to its only NBA title. Walton later paid Lucas the ultimate compliment. He named his first son Lucas after him.

PORTLAND TRAIL BLAZERS

LEGENDS OF THE HARDWOOD

CLYDE DREXLER
SHOOTING GUARD
HEIGHT: 6-FOOT-7
TRAIL BLAZERS SEASONS:
1983–95

A HIGH-FLYING FRATERNITY

The players at the University of Houston in the early 1980s raced up and down the court. They were famous for their explosive slam dunks. A local sportswriter called them Phi Slamma Jama. The name made them sound like they were a fraternity. Another nickname was "Texas's Tallest Fraternity." One of the leaders was 6-foot-7 Clyde Drexler. Drexler continued his high-flying scoring punch when he arrived in Portland. "He was just the best athlete to ever play in Portland," said Blazers forward Steve Jones. "He could make a way when there was no way to be made."

The Blazers won 58 games in the 1977–78 season. That was the best record in the NBA. Walton was named the league's Most Valuable Player (MVP). Fans hoped for back-to-back titles. But the injury bug bit Walton again. He broke his foot early in the playoffs. The Blazers bowed out in the conference semifinals. After that, Walton claimed the team's medical staff hadn't given him proper treatment. He demanded a trade. He didn't get it. He sat out the entire 1978–79 season. Then he signed as a free agent with the San Diego Clippers. He was hurt there, too. "If Bill Walton is healthy, he undoubtedly would go down as one of the five best centers of all time," Petrie said. "There was nobody like him."

THE GLIDE SLIDES INTO PORTLAND

Portland struggled after Walton's departure. They failed to get past the first round of the playoffs in the following four seasons.

Portland struck gold in the 1983 NBA Draft. They chose shooting guard Clyde Drexler. "The Glide," as he was soon called, averaged less than eight points a game as a rookie. He got much better the following season. He averaged nearly 18 points a game. That began a steady rise toward becoming one of the league's top scorers. In the 1985 playoffs, the Blazers stomped the Dallas Mavericks in the first round. But they lost to the Lakers in the conference semifinals. Portland made the playoffs the next four seasons. But each year they couldn't get past the first round.

In the 1989–90 season, Portland won a franchise-best 59 games. The Blazers faced the powerful Detroit Pistons in the NBA Finals. Detroit won four out of five games. All but one game was decided by six points or less. "We had six new people on this team this year, and we reached the NBA Finals," said Drexler. "I just think the future looks so bright."

He was right. The Blazers won 19 of their first 20 games the following season. They finished with 63 victories. But they lost to the Lakers in the Western Conference finals.

Portland returned to the NBA Finals in 1992. They faced the Chicago Bulls. The media billed the series as a matchup between Drexler and Bulls superstar Michael Jordan. Jordan was MVP. Drexler was runner-up. With Chicago leading the series 3–2, Portland took a 15-point lead in Game 6. Chicago surged back for a 97–93 win and the NBA title. "Chicago's defensive intensity picked up, and we didn't handle the ball well," said coach Rick Adelman. "Our guys just ran out of gas."

They also seemed to run out of gas in the next six seasons. They continued to put up winning records. But they continued to lose in the first round of the playoffs. Several key players were traded. The biggest loss came midway through the 1994–95 season. Drexler had been an eight-time All-Star with Portland. Yet the team paid seven players more than they paid him. He demanded a trade. He got it. "Clyde Drexler was the identity of the Portland Trail Blazers, and there will be no substitute," said teammate guard Terry Porter. Porter himself was gone a few months later.

Clyde Drexler

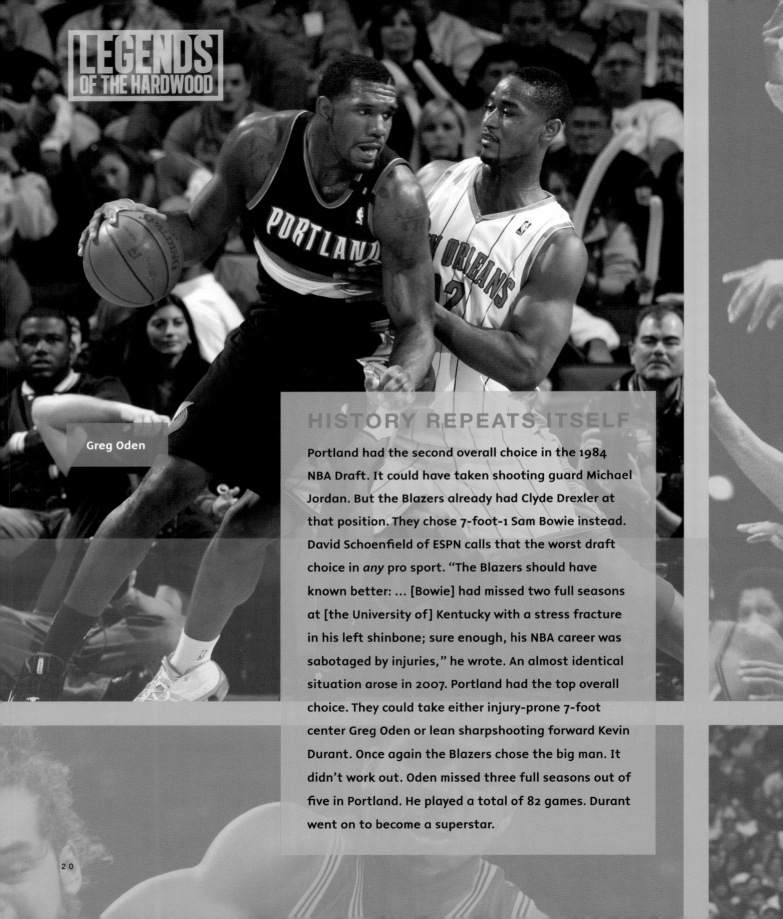

Greg Oden

HISTORY REPEATS ITSELF

Portland had the second overall choice in the 1984 NBA Draft. It could have taken shooting guard Michael Jordan. But the Blazers already had Clyde Drexler at that position. They chose 7-foot-1 Sam Bowie instead. David Schoenfield of ESPN calls that the worst draft choice in *any* pro sport. "The Blazers should have known better: ... [Bowie] had missed two full seasons at [the University of] Kentucky with a stress fracture in his left shinbone; sure enough, his NBA career was sabotaged by injuries," he wrote. An almost identical situation arose in 2007. Portland had the top overall choice. They could take either injury-prone 7-foot center Greg Oden or lean sharpshooting forward Kevin Durant. Once again the Blazers chose the big man. It didn't work out. Oden missed three full seasons out of five in Portland. He played a total of 82 games. Durant went on to become a superstar.

SUCCESS AND STRUGGLES

Portland made another run at the NBA title in the 1998–99 season. By then they had added several new players. The key newcomer was 7-foot-3 center Arvydas Sabonis. "Arvydas and Bill Walton are the two best passing big men ever," said coach Mike Dunleavy. With point guard Damon Stoudamire running the offense, the Blazers soared to the conference finals. But the San Antonio Spurs swept the series.

Portland traded for small forward Scottie Pippen. He had helped the Bulls win six NBA titles. His veteran leadership helped the Blazers return to the conference finals again in 1999–2000. They lost three of the first four games to the Lakers. Portland won the next two. In Game 7, the Blazers built a 15-point lead with just 10 minutes left in the game. Then they fell apart. "Portland choked jumper after jumper, shooting 22 percent for the period," wrote Blazers historian Dave Deckard. "Nobody will forget the sickening feeling of watching that 10 minutes, of seeing the Blazers surrender the biggest Game 7 comeback in playoff history." The Lakers won 89–84.

The Blazers made first-round playoff exits in the next three seasons. They missed the playoffs entirely in 2003–04. That ended 21 straight post-season appearances. It was the second-longest streak in NBA history (The Philadelphia 76ers and San Antonio Spurs both had streaks of 22). The playoffs remained out of reach for four more seasons.

Portland began laying the foundation for better things. They traded for two rookies in the 2006–07 season: power forward LaMarcus Aldridge and shooting guard Brandon Roy. Both were named to the NBA All-Rookie First Team. They helped the Blazers to 32 wins in their first season. The Blazers kept improving. They won 54 games in 2008–09. But they still couldn't get past the first round of the playoffs. This time they lost to the Houston Rockets, 4 games to 2. The next two seasons were almost identical.

Roy had been bothered by knee problems since his college days at the University of Washington. By the end of the 2010–11 season, the stress of long NBA seasons was too much. He retired. Without him, Portland won just 28 games.

RIP CITY RESILIENCE

The Blazers drafted point guard Damian Lillard in 2012. He was the fourth unanimous choice as NBA Rookie of the Year after averaging more than 18 points a game, though the Blazers missed the playoffs again. Lillard, Aldridge, and shooting guard Wesley Matthews sparked the Blazers to a 24–5 start in 2013–14. They finished with 54 wins and made it to the playoffs. The Blazers took a 3–2 series lead over Houston in the first round. But they trailed 98–96 in the final moments of Game 6. A loss would give Houston home-court advantage for the decisive Game 7. Portland had an inbounds play near midcourt with 0.9 seconds remaining. Lillard broke free just outside the three-point line. He caught

Brandon Roy

LAMARCUS ALDRIDGE
POWER FORWARD
HEIGHT: 6-FOOT-11
TRAIL BLAZERS SEASONS: 2006–15

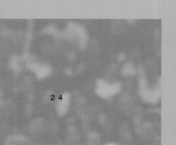

24

YOU GOTTA HAVE HEART

LaMarcus Aldridge had an immediate impact on the Trail Blazers. He was thrust into a starting role shortly after mid-season due to an injury to another player. He was named to the NBA All-Rookie First Team. But with the season almost over, Aldridge had to leave a game and go to the hospital. He was dizzy and his heartbeat was irregular. He was diagnosed with a rare condition known as Wolff-Parkinson-White Syndrome. It affects the rate of heartbeats. Fortunately, it is treatable and hardly ever life-threatening. Within a few years, Aldridge had become one of the league's top forwards and a four-time All-Star. He is the team's all-time leading rebounder (5,434) and third in total points (12,562).

PORTLAND TRAIL BLAZERS

25

the ball and put up a jump shot. The clock read 0:00 as the ball dropped into the net. Portland won 99–98! It is the most famous shot in Blazer history. Mentioning "point-nine" to Blazers fans makes them smile. But San Antonio ended their season in the next round.

Halfway through the 2014–15 season, the Blazers had a scorching 30–11 record. Then Matthews tore his Achilles tendon. He was out for the season. Portland still finished with 51 wins. In the first round of the playoffs, Portland fell to the Memphis Grizzlies. Four starters left following the season. Some were traded. Others became free agents. The most crucial loss was Aldridge. He is Portland's all-time leading rebounder and third-leading scorer.

Many experts thought Portland would be lucky to win 30 games in 2015–16. In January, they seemed to be right. Portland was already seven games under .500. Then Stotts told his team, "I guarantee you guys, if we can be a top-15 ranked defensive team [out of a total of 30] by the end of the season, we will make the playoffs." The players took him up on his guarantee. They finished in a tie for 12th on defense and gained a playoff berth. Third-year shooting guard C. J. McCollum averaged nearly 18 points a game. He and Lillard formed one of the league's most dynamic backcourt combinations. The Blazers beat the Clippers in the first round. They lost in the next round to the defending champion Golden State Warriors, 4 games to 1. Portland held halftime leads in all but one game.

Portland was eliminated in the first round of the playoffs in the next two seasons. After the dramatic series victory over Denver in the second round in 2018–19, the Blazers were swept in the conference finals by the Warriors.

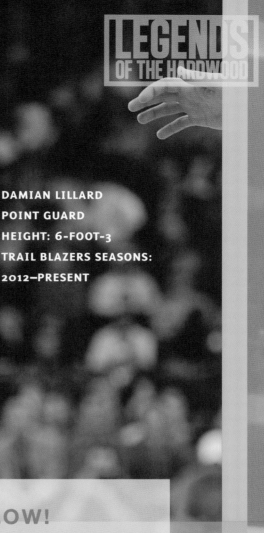

DAMIAN LILLARD
POINT GUARD
HEIGHT: 6-FOOT-3
TRAIL BLAZERS SEASONS:
2012—PRESENT

TWO STARS? TOO LOW!

When Damian Lillard came out of high school, most college recruiting services rated him a two-star player (out of a possible five). Few schools were interested. He chose Weber State University in Utah. Lillard made rapid progress. Before the 2012 NBA Draft, he was considered the country's best point guard prospect. Portland made him the sixth overall choice. He scored 23 points and handed out 11 assists in his first game. Lillard joined Hall of Famers Oscar Robertson and Allen Iverson as the only players with more than 20 points and 10 assists in their debuts. During his Portland career, Lillard became known as "Dame Time" for all the clutch baskets he made. He was a six-time All-Star. In 2021, the NBA named him as one of 75 players on its 75th Anniversary Team.

PORTLAND TRAIL BLAZERS

27

Damian Lillard

Despite a losing record in the COVID-19-shortened 2019–20 season, Portland qualified for the playoffs. They lost to the Lakers in the first round, 4 games to 1. They returned to the winning column the following season, but the result was yet another first-round playoff defeat.

All five of the season-opening starters missed significant parts of the 2021–22 season due to serious injuries or trades. Losing Lillard was especially crucial. He played just 29 games in the early part of the season. The Blazers also traded McCollum shortly after mid-season. Portland lost their last 11 games by an average of more than 22 points a game. The final record of 27–55 meant that the Blazers missed the playoffs for the first time in nine seasons. Anfernee Simons did his best in the absence of Lillard and McCollum. He averaged more than 17 points per game and shot over 40 percent from three-point range. To try to help with the loss of McCollum, Portland drafted shooting guard Shaedon Sharpe with the seventh pick of the 2022 NBA Draft. Also, the Trail Blazers acquired Jerami Grant in an off-season trade with Detroit. He averaged nearly 21 points per game in two seasons with the Pistons.

Rip City fans are among the most loyal and passionate in the NBA. They have been treated to some of the greatest players and performances the league has to offer. Blazermaniacs feel confident that another championship will come to Portland.

Anfernee Simons

INDEX